VOL. 48

CONTENTS

To access audio visit:
www.halleonard.com/mylibrary

Enter Code
1692-3401-8903-1369

Cover photo courtesy of Aerosmith

ISBN 978-0-634-07407-3

HAL•LEONARD®
CORPORATION
7777 W. BLUEMOUND RD. P.O. BOX 13819 MILWAUKEE, WI 53213

Visit Hal Leonard Online at
www.halleonard.com

Back in the Saddle

Words and Music by Steven Tyler and Joe Perry

Tune down 1/2 step:
(low to high) Eb-Ab-Db-Gb-Bb-Eb

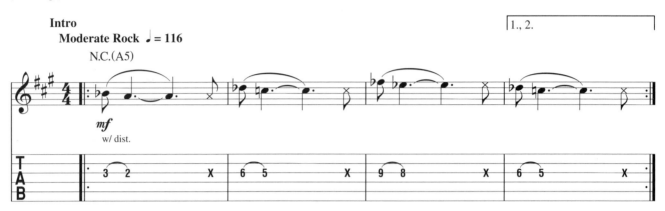

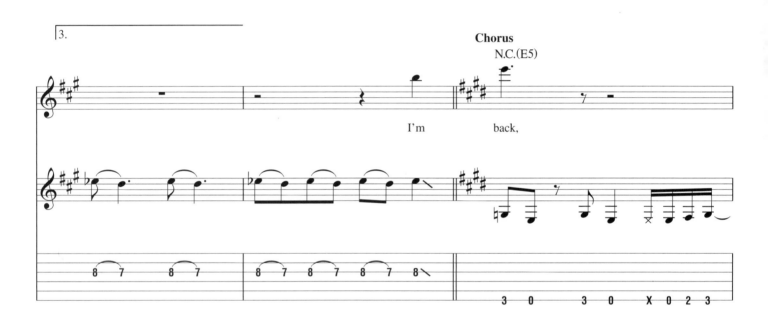

I'm   back,

I'm back   in the sad-dle a - gain. _____   I'm

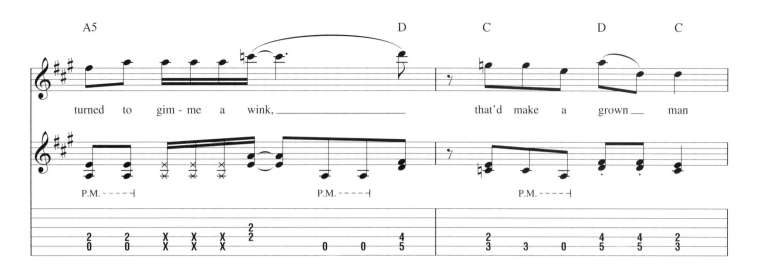

turned to gim-me a wink, _____ that'd make a grown __ man

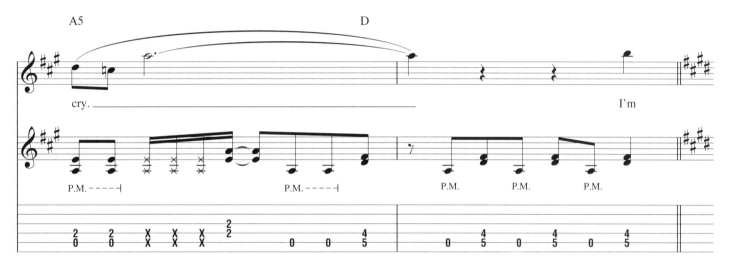

cry. _____ I'm

Chorus

N.C.(E5)

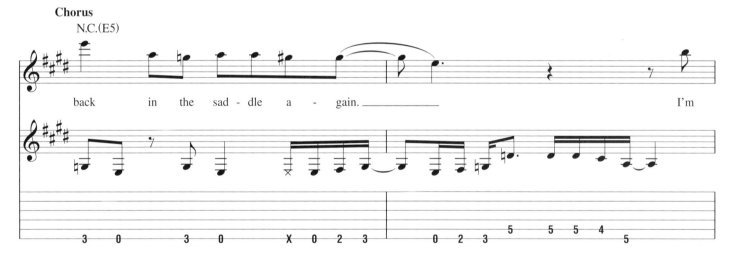

back in the sad-dle a - gain. _____ I'm

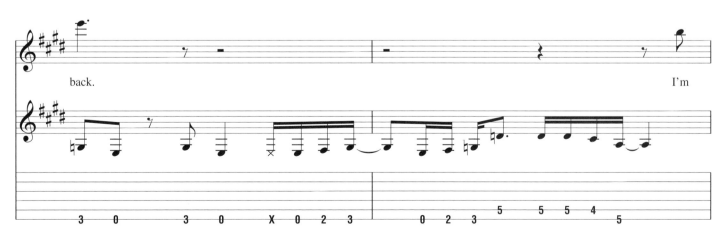

back. _____ I'm

back in the sad - dle a - gain. _____ I'm

back.

Verse

2. Come eas - y, go eas - y, al - right _____ till the ris - in' sun. _____

I'm

the girls are soak - in' wet. __ No tongue's dri - er than mine. __ I'll come when I get

Chorus

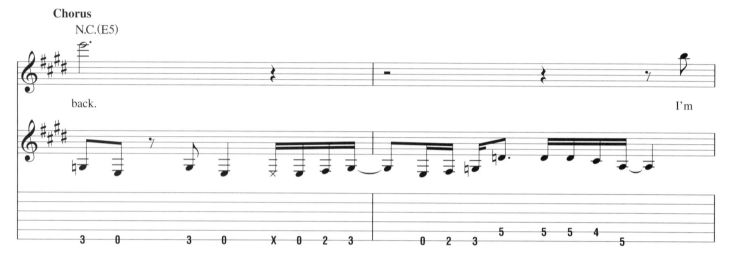

back. I'm

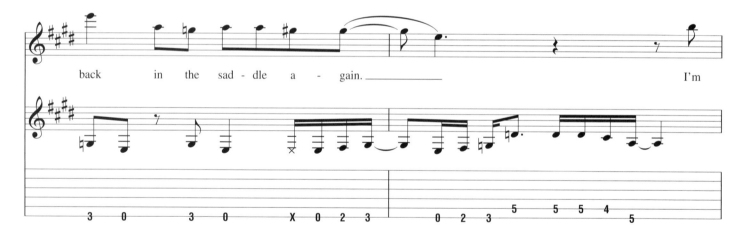

back in the sad - dle a - gain. _____ I'm

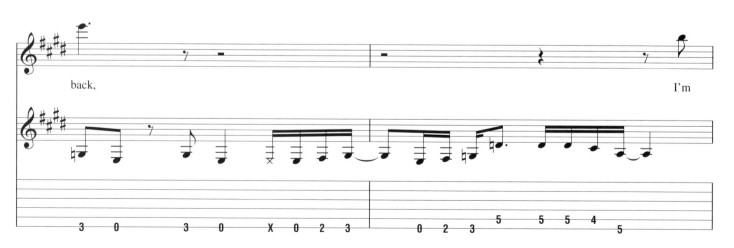

back, I'm

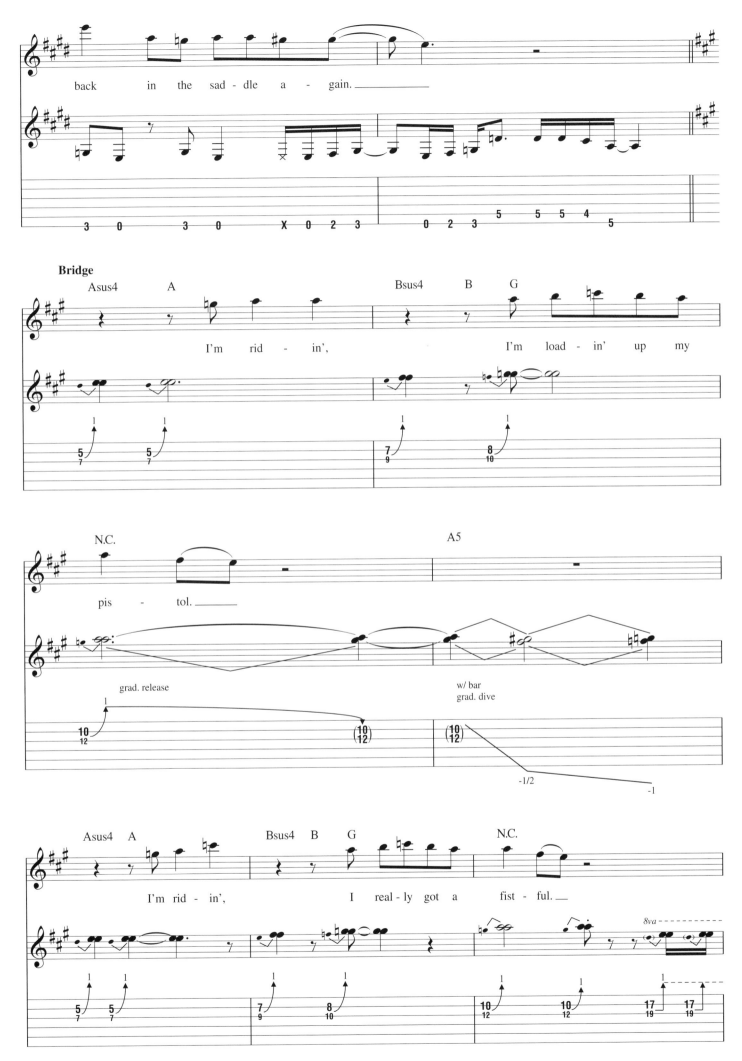

Outro

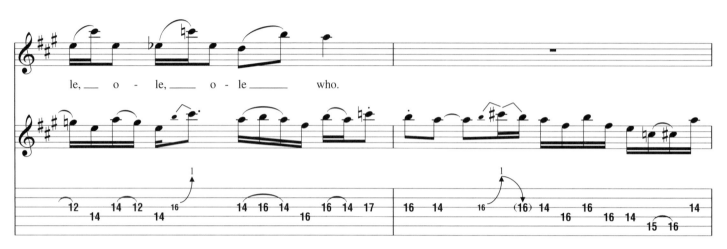

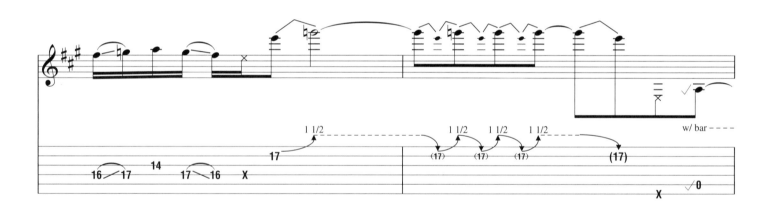

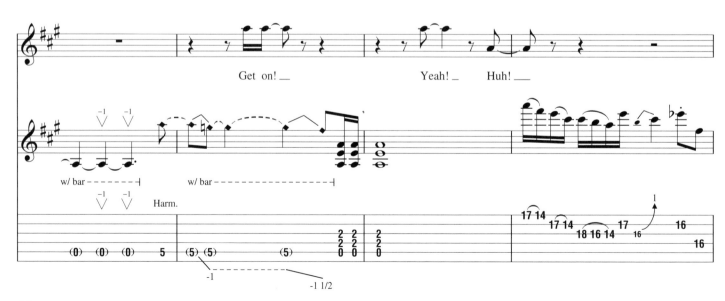

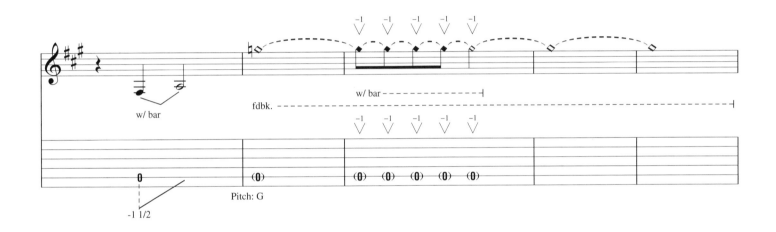

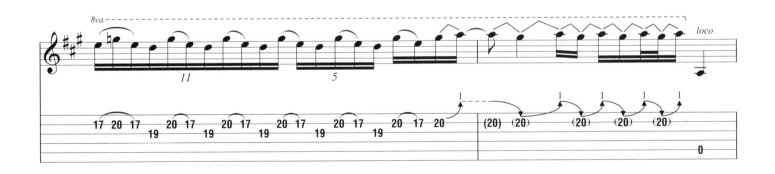

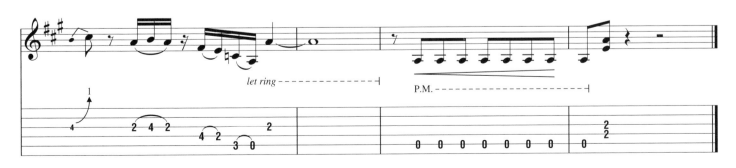

Draw the Line

Words and Music by Steven Tyler and Joe Perry

when to draw the line.

Interlude

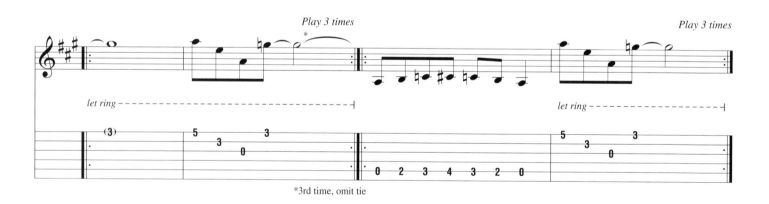

*3rd time, omit tie

Bridge

E5

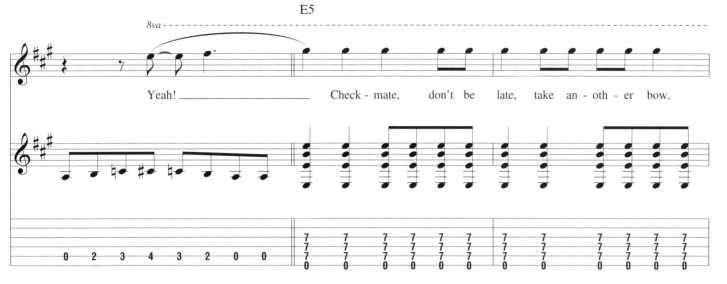

Yeah! _____ Check - mate, don't be late, take an - oth - er bow.

That's right, im - pos - si - ble when you got to be your- self. You're the boss, _

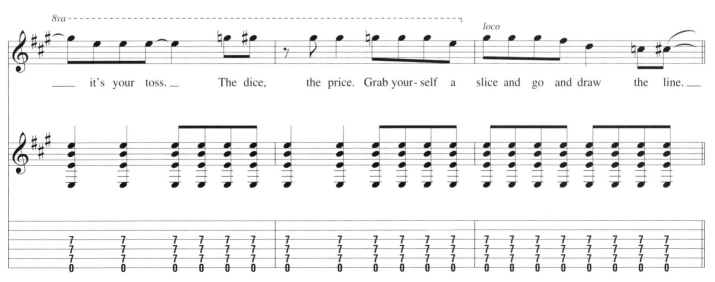

___ it's your toss. _ The dice, the price. Grab your- self a slice and go and draw the line. _

Outro

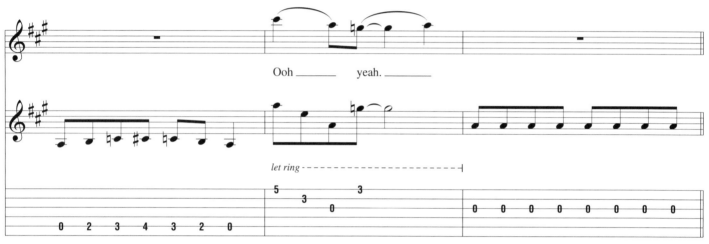

Additional Lyrics

2. The Indian Summer, Carrie was all over the floor.
   She was a wet net winner and rarely ever left the store.
   She'd sing and dance all night, and wrong all the right outta me.
   Oh, pass me the vial and cross your fingers, it don't take time.
   Know where to draw the line.

Mama Kin

Words and Music by Steven Tyler

E5

for - get to drop me a line.

Said, you're as

Pre-Chorus

2nd time, substitute Fill 1

A5   E5   A7   E5

bald   as an egg at eight - een, ___   an' work - in' for your dad is just a ___

1/4

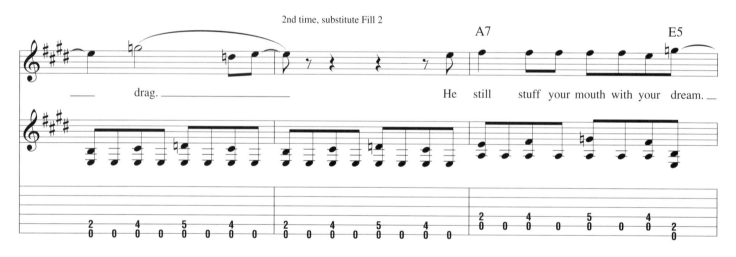

2nd time, substitute Fill 2

A7   E5

___   drag. _____   He still   stuff your mouth with your dream. ___

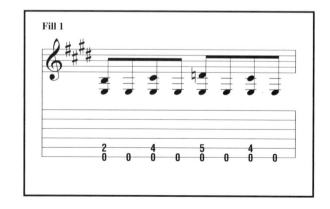

Fill 1

Fill 2

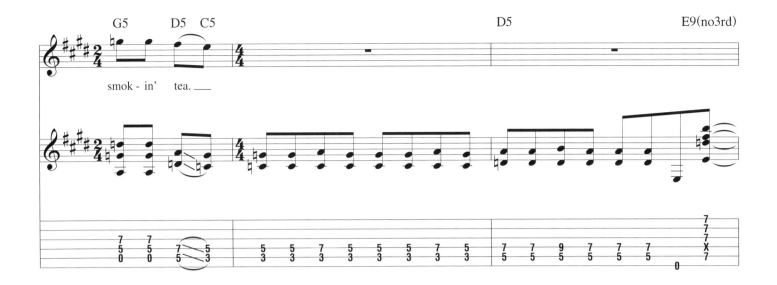

smok - in' tea. ____

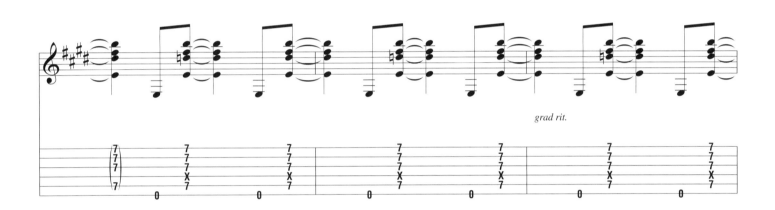

grad rit.

Freely

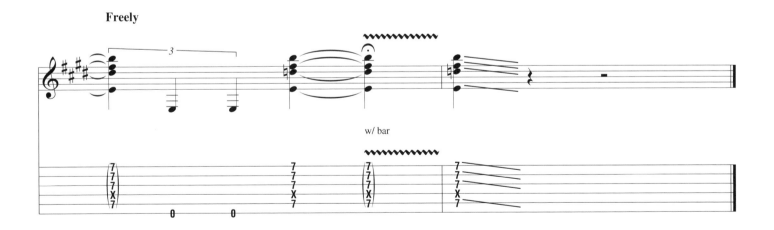

w/ bar

Additional Lyrics

2. Yeah, it ain't easy, livin' like you wanna.
    And it's so hard ta find peac eof mind. Yes, it is.
    The way I see it, you gotta say shit,
    But don't forget to drop me a line.

Dream On

Words and Music by Steven Tyler

may-be to-mor-row the good Lord will take you a-way.

To Coda ⊕

Interlude

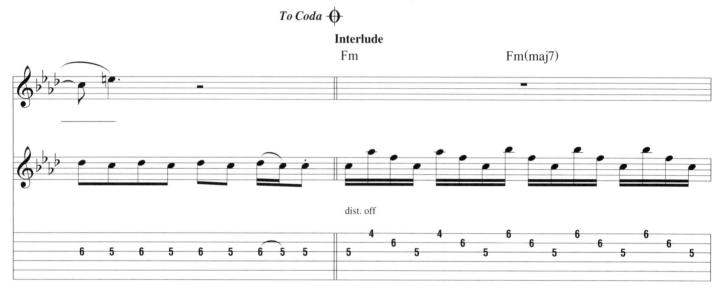

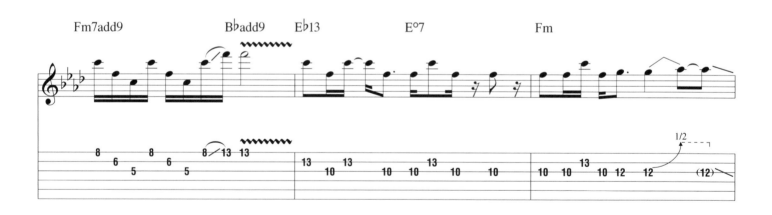

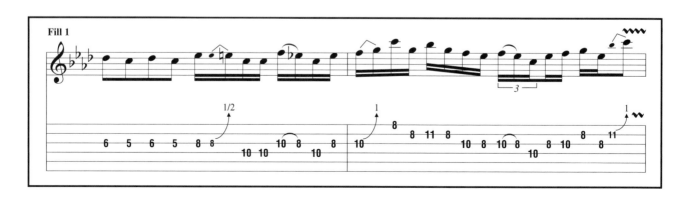

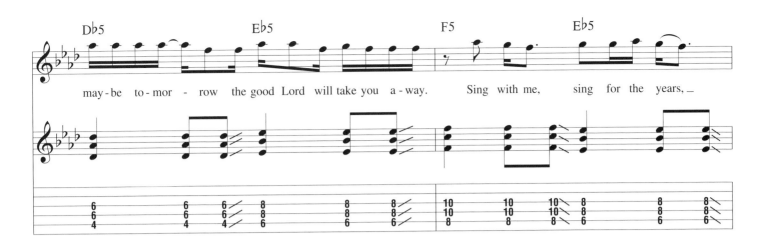

may-be to-mor - row the good Lord will take you a - way. Sing with me, sing for the years, _

sing for the laugh-ter 'n' sing _ for the tears. _ Sing _ with me if it's just for to - day, _

may-be to-mor - row the good Lord will take you a - way. _____

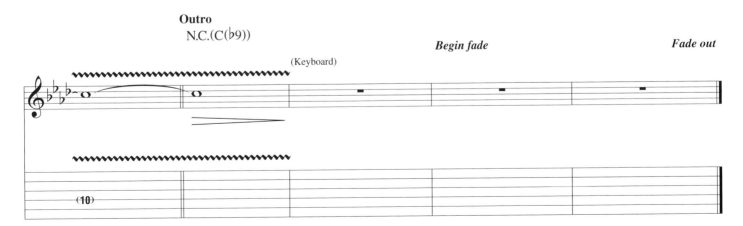

Outro
N.C.(C(♭9))

Begin fade   *Fade out*

(Keyboard)

Last Child

Words and Music by Steven Tyler and Brad Whitford

Tune down 1/2 step:
(low to high) E♭-A♭-D♭-G♭-B♭-E♭

Intro
Moderately slow ♩ = 80

Verse

1. Take ___ me back ___ to ah, South Tal - la - has - see,
2. *See additional lyrics*

down 'cross the bridge _ to my sweet sas - sa - fras - sy.

Can't ___ stand _ up ___ on my feet in the cit - y.

Got ___ to get back _ to the real nit - ty grit - ty.

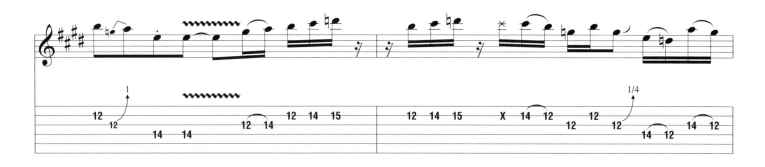

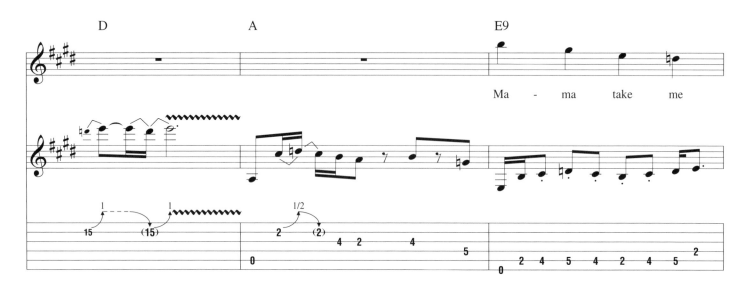

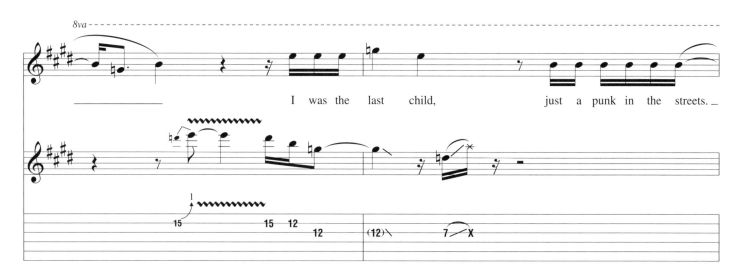

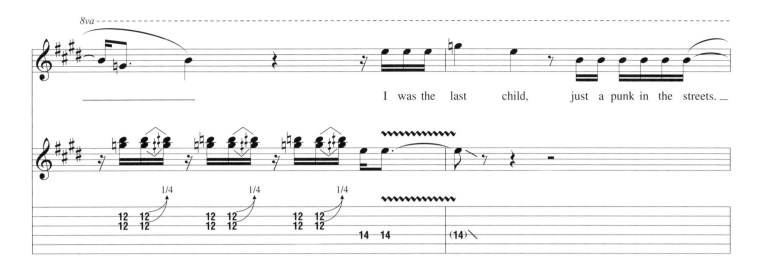

I was the last child, just a punk in the streets.

Begin fade

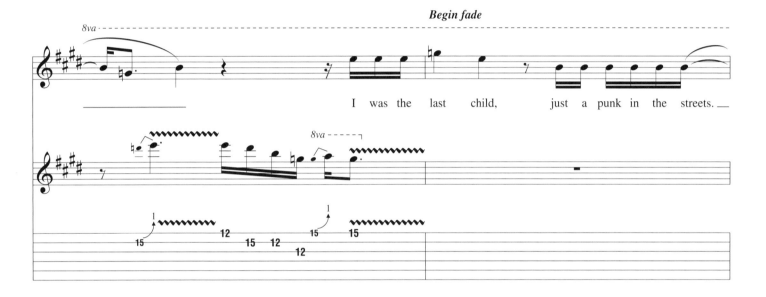

I was the last child, just a punk in the streets.

Fade out

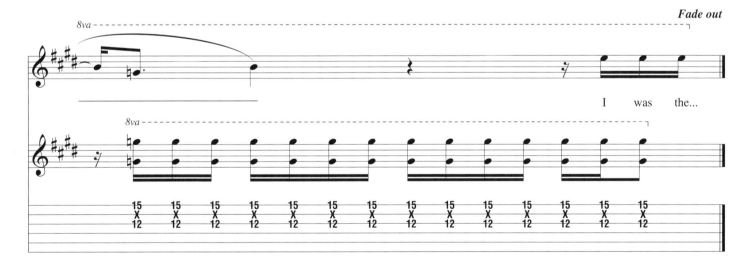

I was the...

Additional Lyrics

2. Get out in the field, put the mule in the stable.
   Ma, she's a-cookin', put the eats on the table.
   Hate's in the city and my love's in the meadow.
   Hands on the plough and my feet's in the ghetto.

Pre-Chorus 2. Stand up, sit down, don't do nothin'.
   It ain't no good when boss man's stuffin' it down their throats
   For paper notes and their babies cry while cities lie at their feet,
   When you're rockin' the streets.

Same Old Song and Dance

Words and Music by Steven Tyler and Joe Perry

old song and dance — my friend. — It's the same —

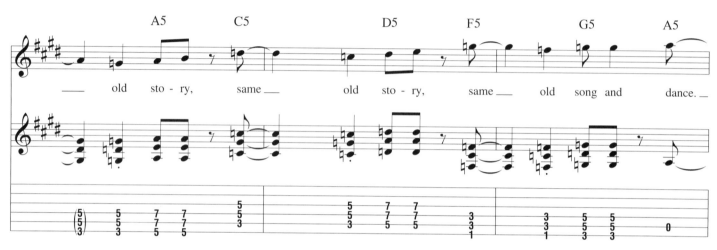

old sto-ry, same — old sto-ry, same — old song and dance. —

Guitar Solo

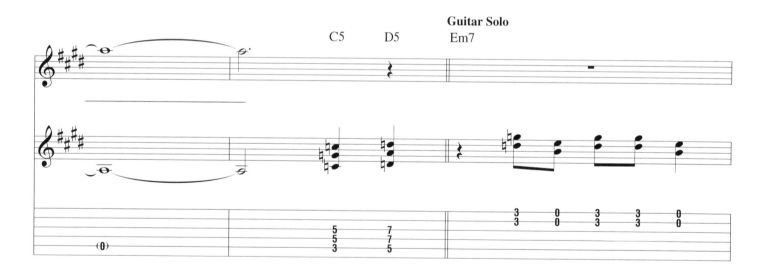

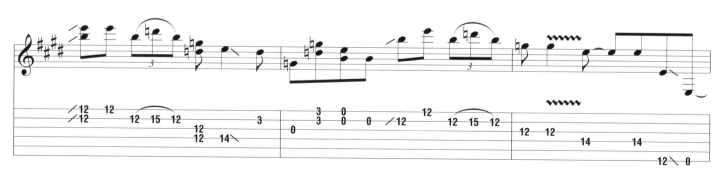

Bridge

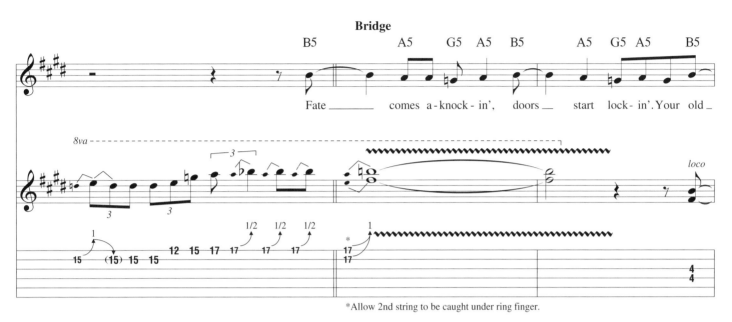

*Allow 2nd string to be caught under ring finger.

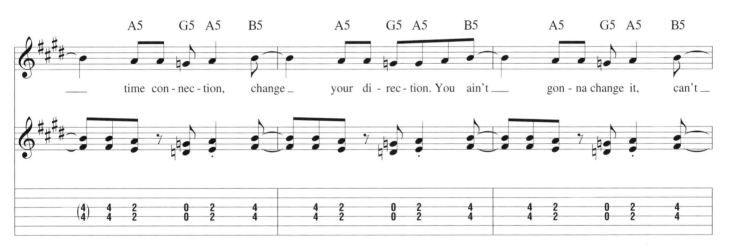

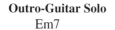

Outro-Guitar Solo

Em7

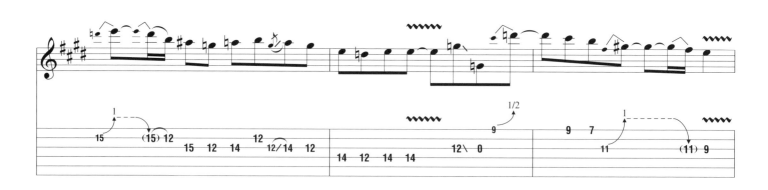

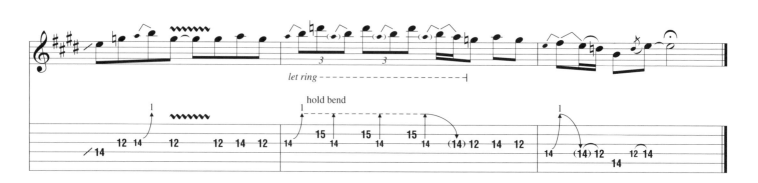

Additional Lyrics

3. When you're low down and dirty
   From walking the street
   With your old hurdy gurdy,
   No one to meet.
   Say love ain't the same on the south side o' town.
   You could look but you ain't gonna find it around.

Walk This Way

Words and Music by Steven Tyler and Joe Perry

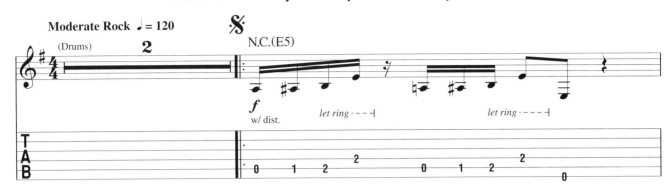

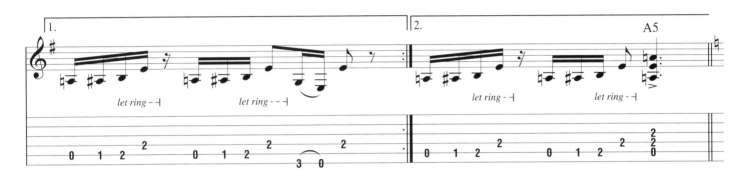

Verse

1. Back-stroke lov-er al-ways hid-in''neath the cov-ers, "Gon-na talk to you,"my dad-dy say, _ said, "You
3. *See additional lyrics*

ain't seen noth-in' till you're down on a muf-fin and you're sure to be a chang-in' your ways." _ I met a

cheer - lead - er, was a real young bleed - er all the times I could rem - i - nisce, __ 'cause the

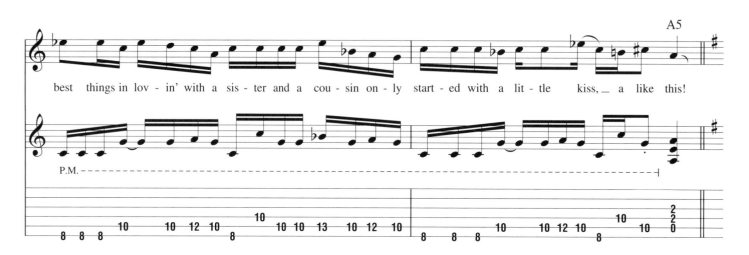

best things in lov - in' with a sis - ter and a cou - sin on - ly start - ed with a lit - tle kiss, __ a like this!

Interlude

Verse

2., 4. See - saw swing - in' with the boys in the school and your feet fly - in' up in the air, __ I sing,

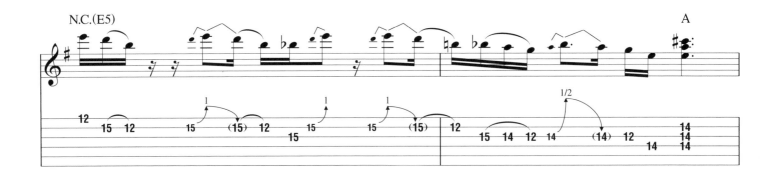

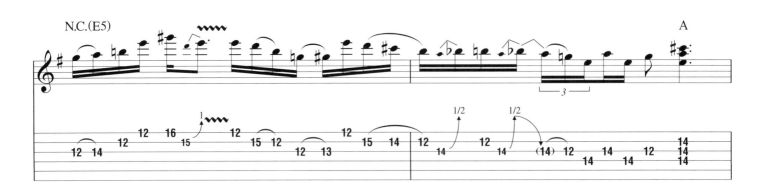

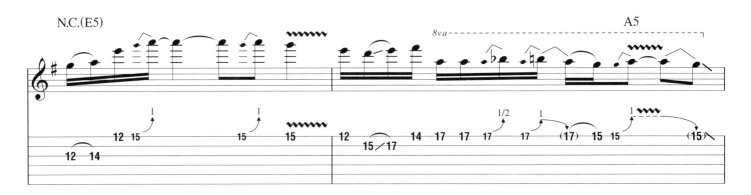

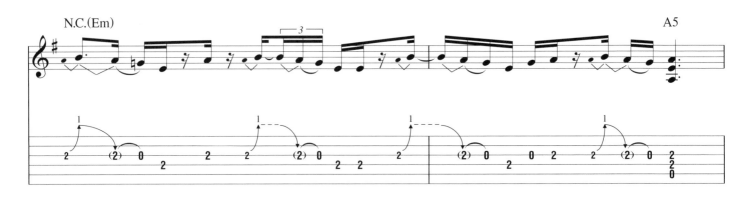

Begin fade

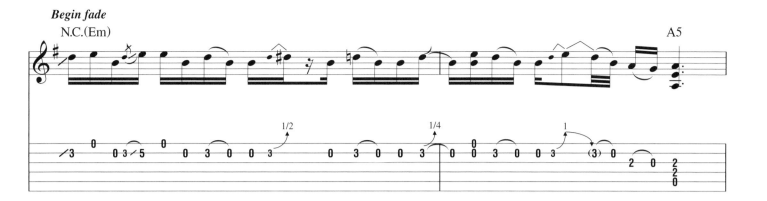

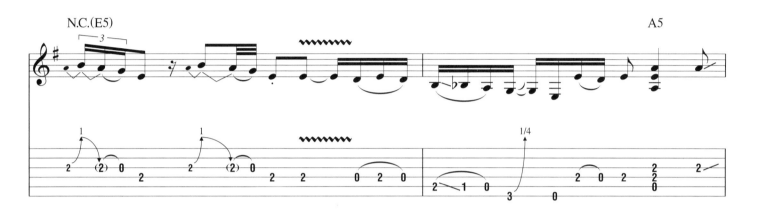

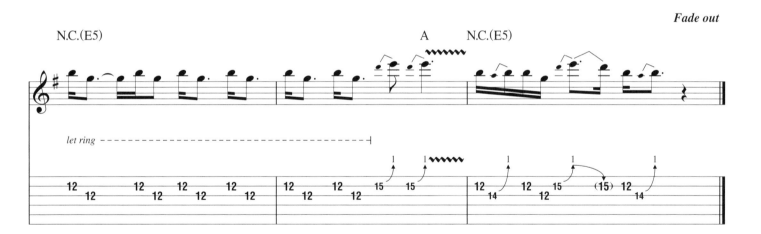

Additional Lyrics

3. School girl skinny with a classy kind a sassy little skirt's climbin' way up her knee,
There was three young ladies in the school gym locker when I noticed they was lookin' at me.
I was in high school loser, never made it with a lady till the boys told me somethin' I missed,
Then my next door neighbor with a daughter had a favor so I gave her just a little kiss, a like this!

Sweet Emotion

Words and Music by Steven Tyler and Tom Hamilton

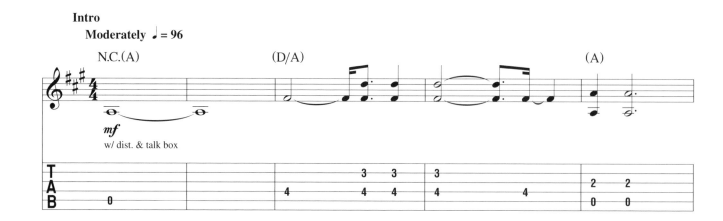

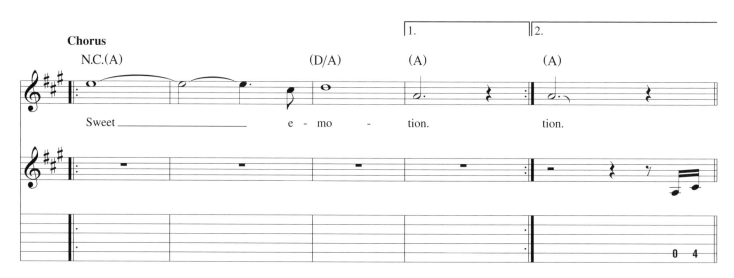

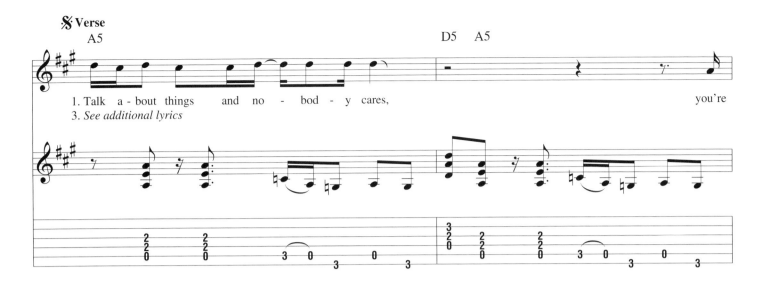

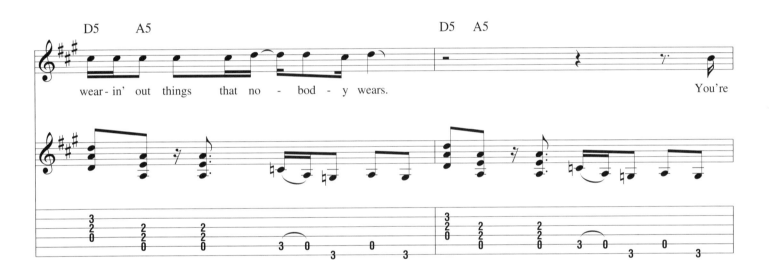

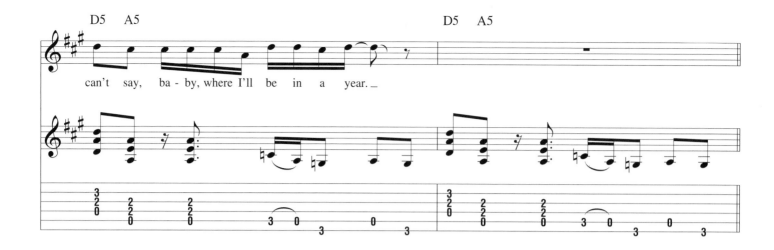

can't say, ba - by, where I'll be in a year.

Interlude

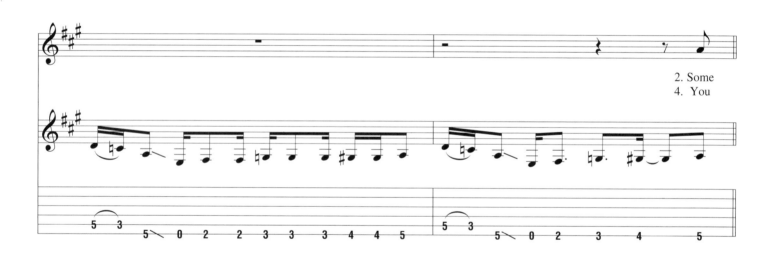

2. Some
4. You

said my

Verse

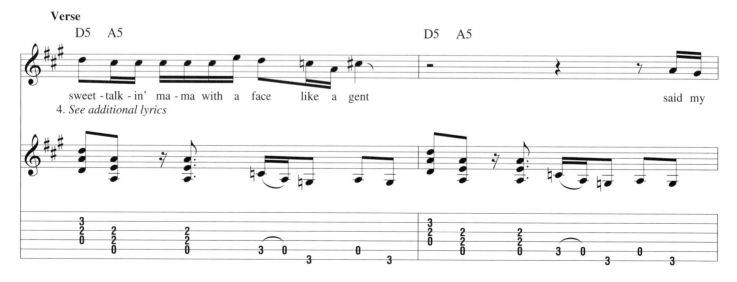

sweet - talk - in' ma - ma with a face like a gent
4. *See additional lyrics*

get up and go _____ must-'ve got up and went. _____   Well, I

got good news, she's a real ___ good li - ar,   'cause my

back - stage boo - gie, set yo' pants on fire.

Interlude

N.C.

Play 3 times

67

Chorus

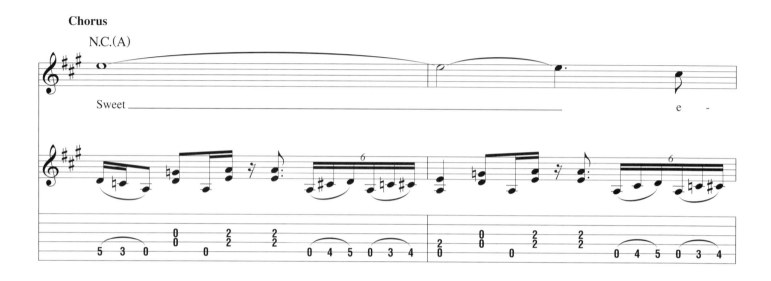

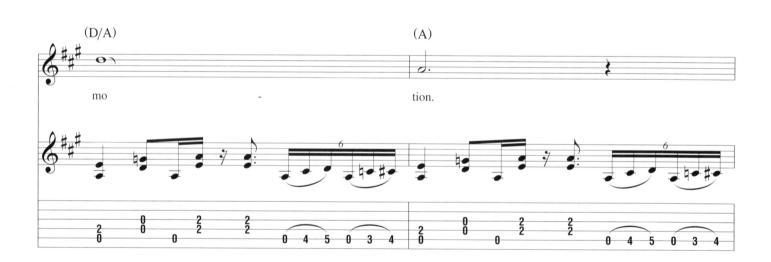

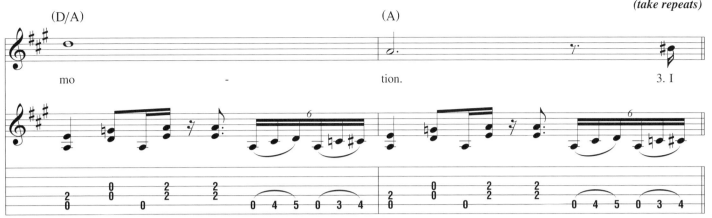

Coda

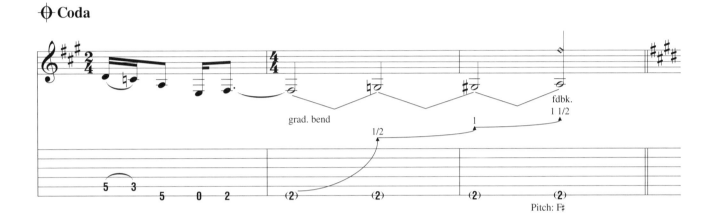

Outro-Guitar Solo

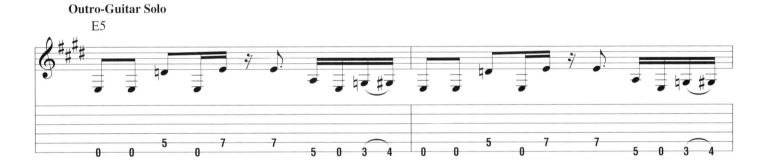

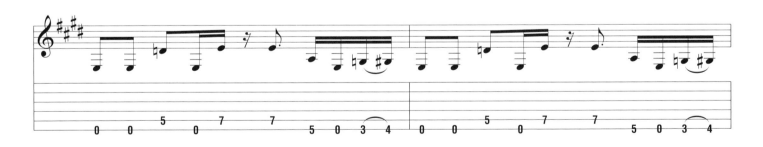

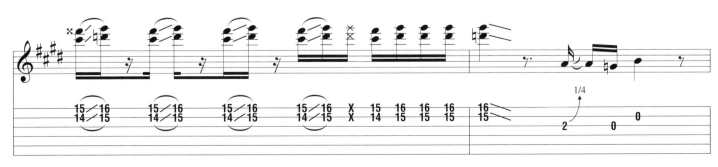

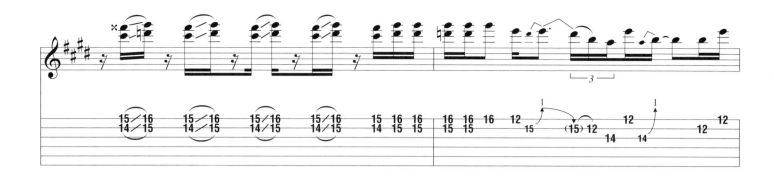

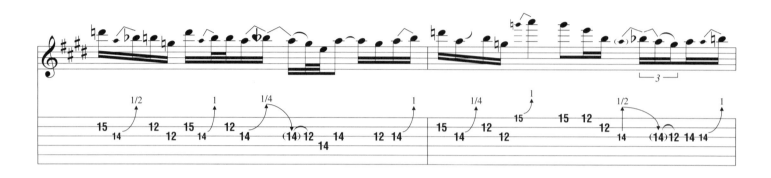

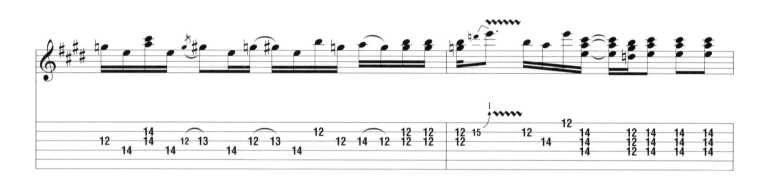

Begin fade

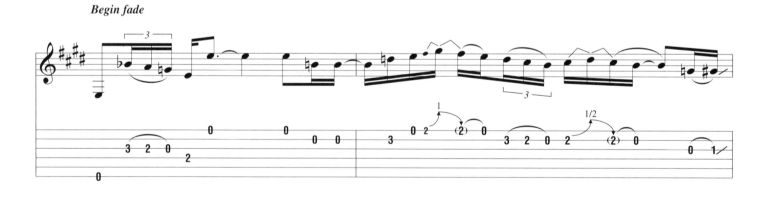

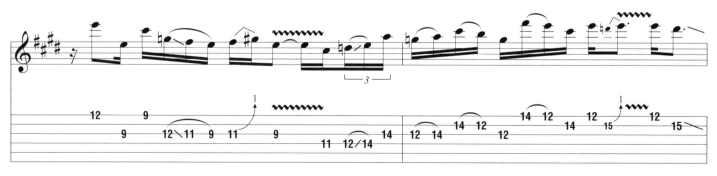

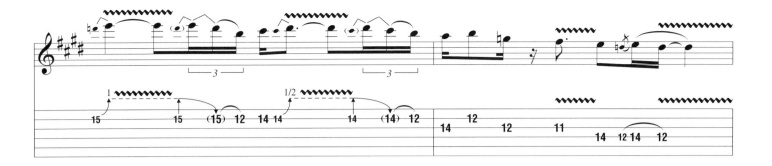

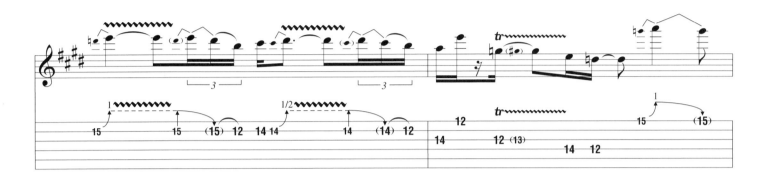

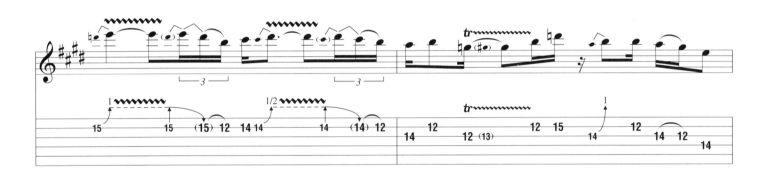

Fade out

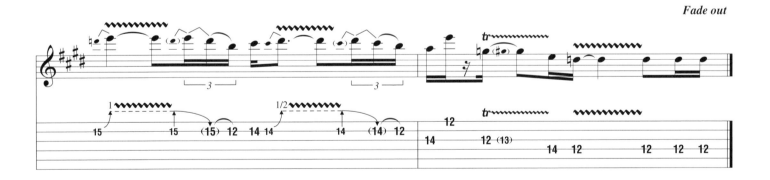

Additional Lyrics

3. I pulled into town in a police car,
   Your daddy said I took you just a little too far.
   You're tellin' me things but your girlfriend lied,
   You can't catch me 'cause the rabbit done died.
   Yes, it did!

4. You stand in the front just a shakin' yo ass,
   I'll take you backstage, you can drink from my glass.
   I'm talkin' 'bout somethin' you can sure understand,
   'Cause a month on the road and I'll be eatin' from your hand.

GUITAR NOTATION LEGEND

THE MUSICAL STAFF shows pitches and rhythms and is divided by bar lines into measures. Pitches are named after the first seven letters of the alphabet.

TABLATURE graphically represents the guitar fingerboard. Each horizontal line represents a string, and each number represents a fret.

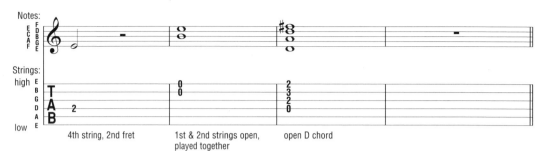

4th string, 2nd fret

1st & 2nd strings open, played together

open D chord

HALF-STEP BEND: Strike the note and bend up 1/2 step.

WHOLE-STEP BEND: Strike the note and bend up one step.

GRACE NOTE BEND: Strike the note and immediately bend up as indicated.

SLIGHT (MICROTONE) BEND: Strike the note and bend up 1/4 step.

BEND AND RELEASE: Strike the note and bend up as indicated, then release back to the original note. Only the first note is struck.

PRE-BEND: Bend the note as indicated, then strike it.

VIBRATO: The string is vibrated by rapidly bending and releasing the note with the fretting hand.

PALM MUTING: The note is partially muted by the pick hand lightly touching the string(s) just before the bridge.

HAMMER-ON: Strike the first (lower) note with one finger, then sound the higher note (on the same string) with another finger by fretting it without picking.

PULL-OFF: Place both fingers on the notes to be sounded. Strike the first note and without picking, pull the finger off to sound the second (lower) note.

LEGATO SLIDE: Strike the first note and then slide the same fret-hand finger up or down to the second note. The second note is not struck.

SHIFT SLIDE: Same as legato slide, except the second note is struck.

TRILL: Very rapidly alternate between the notes indicated by continuously hammering on and pulling off.

TAPPING: Hammer ("tap") the fret indicated with the pick-hand index or middle finger and pull off to the note fretted by the fret hand.

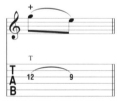

NATURAL HARMONIC: Strike the note while the fret-hand lightly touches the string directly over the fret indicated.

PINCH HARMONIC: The note is fretted normally and a harmonic is produced by adding the edge of the thumb or the tip of the index finger of the pick hand to the normal pick attack.

TREMOLO PICKING: The note is picked as rapidly and continuously as possible.

VIBRATO BAR DIVE AND RETURN: The pitch of the note or chord is dropped a specified number of steps (in rhythm), then returned to the original pitch.

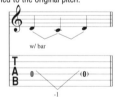

VIBRATO BAR SCOOP: Depress the bar just before striking the note, then quickly release the bar.

VIBRATO BAR DIP: Strike the note and then immediately drop a specified number of steps, then release back to the original pitch.

Additional Musical Definitions

(accent) • Accentuate note (play it louder).

(staccato) • Play the note short.

D.S. al Coda • Go back to the sign (%), then play until the measure marked "***To Coda***," then skip to the section labelled "**Coda**."

D.C. al Fine • Go back to the beginning of the song and play until the measure marked "***Fine***" (end).

Fill • Label used to identify a brief melodic figure which is to be inserted into the arrangement.

N.C. • Harmony is implied.

• Repeat measures between signs.

• When a repeated section has different endings, play the first ending only the first time and the second ending only the second time.